Tales from the Crib
Poetic Tales of Childhood Misfortune and Redemption

Tales from the Crib
Poetic Tales of Childhood Misfortune and Redemption

Eric Manning

Tales from the Crib
Poetic Tales of Childhood Misfortune
and Redemption

ISBN – 9798991625449

Table of Contents

Introduction

I will tell you some tales,
Some tales from the crib.
It starts with lives of children,
Placed in a highchair, without a bib.

How do unfortunate lives get started?
Would you ever dare to know?
First relationships lead them to darkness,
Despite a desire to love and grow.

Prelude: The Dark Cloud Surrounds

Just what is this dark cloud,
And what does it do?
How does it affect these innocent children,
Which distorts reality and all that is true?

Chapter 1: Len and the Jack

Let's start out the tales
With a boy named Len.
Who is stuck inside a world
He wished he'd never been.

Len loved to crank his jack-in-the-box,
This happened day and night.
But each time he did this,
Out came a demon of fright.

He kept on cranking the jack-in-the-box,
Hoping to see a kind face that was true.
But every time it popped out,
It scared him and left him blue.

The Jack reminded him of the dread he felt,
When he looked into his father's eyes.
He gripped the bars of the crib and saw,
An ugly face of despise.

He began to dread the time,
His father came home from work.
The disappointed voice would call,
From downstairs where he did lurk.

His father bragged about his great talents,
His intellect and aspirations in life.
He never cared about his own son's needs,
Nor the needs of his wife.

Often things happened at Len's house,
That stirred his father's rage.
Len tried to escape his crib,
Like an animal trapped in a cage.

Len noticed this especially when
Father's work went wrong in the house.
Then he became afraid of his rage,
And tried to be quiet as a mouse.

When he heard his parents' yelling,
They were headed for a fight.
There was little hope for love,
And his days turned into night.

Len knew his resentful father,
Was sure to come back around.
To take out his frustrations,
By smashing him to the ground.

When he cried for his mother's protection,
Her mind was too far away.
She was often too angry to help him.
Would he ever survive the day?

After so many days went by,
He realized there was no escape.
The dark cloud of fear surrounded him,
Hopelessness caused his heart to break.

Chapter 2: For Children's Snake

Here is another tale.

The tale of Jemma and Nate.

Before they knew their own names,

They were trapped under a snake.

The snake slithered into their crib,
He was cunning and didn't make a sound.
They cried out to their parents for help,
…But they never came around.

Their parents were oblivious,
And paid them no mind.
When the kids cried for attention,
They got a "wack" on the behind!

Jemma and Nate had many needs,
With a strong desire to be hugged.
When these needs were brought to light,
Their parents frowned and shrugged.

Their father was too busy at work,
He didn't care about what they need.
Also, his wife was quite unhappy,
But this truth he did not heed.

"Why don't you care!"
The mother would say.
With apathetic eyes,
He just walked away.

The mother soon realized,
She was all alone.
The man in her house,
Had a cold heart of stone.

The kid's parents grew more distant,
Each and every day.
Never caring who they were,
Or if they were okay.

The snake saw how oblivious
The parents were to his game.
Now, he could slither in,
Without them even knowing his name.

So closer and closer he slid,
Into the family's life.
The father never noticed,
Not even his wife.

Despite the children's cry for help,
In such a desperate time,
The snake looked up to the heavens and said,
"Now they are mine!"

Chapter 3: Mother Viper

There once was a wicked mother,
Who raised a boy so young.
One day he saw evil come,
From the tip of his mother's tongue.

Enrique was a young child,
He could never understand.
Where did her anger come from?
Or why she smacked him with her hand?

He thought to himself,
"Just what did I say?"
Mom became angry and struck me,
Before I could get out of the way.

At first Enrique cried out,
But learned that no one would care.
He developed a numbness inside him,
Because the pain was too much to bear.

Although he tried his best
To avoid his mother's rage,
He was often trapped in his crib,
Like an animal in a cage.

He outgrew his baby clothes,
And became an older child.
He perceived his mother's tongue
To be like a viper in the wild.

Many times, he tried to pull
The covers over his head.
When he heard his mother screaming,
He knew he'd be better off dead.

No matter how he tried,
To avoid her screeching shout,
She injected her poison, deep in his soul.
Traumatizing him without a doubt.

As he grew older, he went to school,
And tried his best to relate.
But the venom inside ran so deep,
That he could never escape.

Chapter 4: Franken-Pa

Jimi longed for time
    with grandpa,
Just to get to know
    him.
Every time Jimi saw
    his face,
His expression was
    quite grim.

Sometimes, Jimi
    followed,
To see where grandpa
    would go.
But when Jimi
    approached him,
His resentment would surely show.

So, Jimi watched and waited,
To connect at the right time.
But grandpa always frowned at him,
With a face as bitter as a lime.

Jimi went to the field with him,
To help him bail some hay.
But that was never good enough;
Grandpa rejected him, every day.

As more time went by,
without talking to his kin,
He realized he was resented.
Everything he did was like a sin.

Eventually Jimi realized
He could do nothing right.
His grandpa always despised him,
Whenever he was in his sight.

So, Jimi started to hate
Being with grandpa at all.
If he dared try to know him,
He was headed for a fall.

After many days had passed,
Grandpa saw Jimi's hate as well.
He was offended and attacked him,
Like Frankenstein under a spell.

Jimi grew older and wiser,
And he knew it was just too late.
The relationship with grandpa
was full of resentment and hate.

Jimi finally gave up,
And looked up to the sky.
Why did he turn into "Franken-pa"?
But Jimi never knew why.

Chapter 5: Gram-Zombie

Jimi had a baby sister,

Her parents named her Shanay.

He was worried sick about her,

When she was with Gramma each day.

His sister was a blessing to him;
Her face shined like the sun.
But he knew Gram-Zombie would hurt her,
Quicker than the sound of a gun.

Oh yes, Jimi saw her dark side,
Come out many times before.
One time her one-eyed cat disobeyed,
And she smacked it onto the floor.

Grams had a pudgy little dog,
That looked so fluffy and cute.
But whenever he did not obey her,
She kicked him like a brute.

Jimi and Shannay always wanted
To pet grams fluffy dog.
But when they tried, he bit them,
Like a vicious, wild hog.

The children tried to talk with Grams,
But the day turned into night.
She couldn't hold back her madness for long,
And gave them a horrible fright.

She even prayed with the children,
Each night before bed.
But that was just deception,
To hide Gram-Zombie of the Living Dead.

She even preached her Bible to them,
While in the light of day.
But her unresolved issues haunted them,
If she did not get her way.

One day Gram's husband, Franken-Pa,
Developed an illness in his head.
The children saw her get mad,
And tie him to his bed.

They looked across the room at him,
And wondered, "How could this be?"
They couldn't believe their eyes,
As he struggled to get free.

They watched wide eyed and leery,
As he kicked up the sheets of his bed.
They feared Grams would attack him,
With her raging fists of dread.

She looked out from the kitchen,
To ask if he wanted to eat.
She saw him breaking free,
As he tried to get to his feet.

Grams could no longer wear
Her sweet old lady disguise.
Her zombie came out with a vengeance!
She beat him; his life she despised.

It was now obvious to the children,
Their grandparents' issues did linger.
They looked at Grams with terror,
She had death in her eyes... and a broken
   finger.

Chapter 6: Tasty and Flapjack

A child was conceived,
In a land far away.
His parents were not found,
Not even in the light of day.

Where he would end up,
No one would know.
The cold cruel wind,
was certain to blow.

He ended up in a home,
where he should not have been.
Nobody protected him,
Up until the age of ten.

Left alone, he wandered the streets,
Looking for acceptance and love.
But he came home feeling empty,
With no sign of hope from above.

Many days the child went hungry,
And was always looking for a treat.
All he could find was anger and chaos,
While walking, out on the street.

After searching for days,
In the hot blazing sun,
He found a woman to care for him,
But her man carried a gun.

He said to the child, "Have whatever you
    want,"
"But you must deliver my drugs."
"Sweet mama will take care of you,"
"And give you plenty of hugs".

So, the woman then
Took the child by the hand.
She looked him in the eyes, and said,
"Can you be my brave little man?"

Right then and there,
He fell into a trance.
With stars in his eyes,
He was willing to take a chance.

He thought she was an angel,
Sent from God above.
But she led him to her bed,
And told him it was love.

After it was over,

He saw a twinkle in her eye.

"You're my tasty little snack," she said,

"A slice of sweet Georgia pie!"

Mesmerized by her affection,
He was empowered by her love.
With pride he shouted, "My name is Tasty!"
"To hell with my family, I will rise above!"

Her man had a big smile,
And gave Tasty a high five.
"You've become my little man!"
"Now take this gun to stay alive."

Tasty had a new life now,
Running drugs on the street.
He made lots of cash,
And he never missed a beat.

His older brother, Flapjack,
Saw him doing quite well.
He became so full of envy,
He had to give him hell.

Tasty tried to hang out
With his brother and his friends.
They beat him and locked him in a box,
And yelled, "This is where your life ends!"

Many hours passed by,
And no one heard him scream.
His brother wouldn't tell where he was,
For he was much too mean.

Sweet Mama walked the streets that day,
Looking to make score.
She heard a little boy screaming,
And crying like never before.

She thought to herself,
"That sounds familiar to me."
But what do I know?
I just have to let this be.

She walked the boulevard,
Not a soul in sight.
She still heard the familiar
   cry,
Of the voice in the night.

She tried to ignore the voice,
But could not let it go.
She followed the desperate
   cries,
As the wicked wind began to
   blow.

She turned some corners and
Went down a dead-end
   street.
She finally found the voice,
It was Tasty she came to
   greet.

Sweet Mama cried out,
"Oh my god, baby, are you ok?"
"I wondered why you weren't around."
"I hadn't seen you the whole day!"

"Over here!", Tasty cried,
"I'm inside a box!"
She turned and ran to him
and broke off the locks.

She lifted him out and set him free,
As he let out an angry shout.
As he began to desperately weep,
She cared for him without a doubt.

Tasty wrapped his arms
Around his new sweet mama.
She looked him in the eyes and said,
"You're safe from all the drama."

She took him home and put him to bed.
Tasty slept for the rest of the night.
When he woke the next day, he knew
Something was just not right.

Flapjack's abuse penetrated,
Deep inside his heart.
Now he knew why he hated his brother,
Right from the start.

Many times, his brother abused him.
No one would hear his cry.
Tasty became so sad and lost,
That he now just wanted to die.

He had to do what her man said,
Or he would have to leave.
He knew he would lose his new mama,
And this he would surely grieve.

Back into the wild,
Tasty then went.
Delivering drugs in dangerous places,
Every dollar he made was already spent.

Tasty thought he had finally
Arrived at the promised land.
He found somebody to love, until
He was threatened by a gun in a hand.

Tasty and a friend
were out on a run.
Their world turned dark
When they had to use a gun.

A customer's face lit up
With an angry and evil glow.
He growled, "I've been cheated son,"
"Someone has to die; don't you know?"

Tasty's whole life
flashed right before his eyes.
The angry man approached them,
Both of whom, he did despise.

As the man made his move,
Toward his fateful friend,
He pistol-whipped him so hard
Tasty thought it was the end.

Tasty quickly stood up, alarmed,
From the other side of the room.
Pulling his gun from the back of his pants
He shot the man. Sent him to his doom.

The neighbor next door called the cops,
He heard the forty-five.
Tasty knew he had to kill,
To keep them both alive.

Tasty and his friend panicked in fear,
They bolted out the door.
Before they knew it, they were slammed,
Onto a cold hard concrete floor.

The cops slapped on the cuffs,
And took them both to jail.
Tasty was waiting for his trial,
Held without any bail.

Alone in his cell,
He wondered when,
He would see his adored
Sweet Mama, ever again.

Tasty got a lawyer,
Who represented quite well.
The judge ruled "self-defense."
He was freed from life in a prison cell.

When he finally got home, he ran right back
To see his sweet mama again.
But she was out working, walking the streets,
He knew she'd be back, but when?

She finally got home,
about quarter to four.
Drugged out of her mind,
She dragged herself through the door.

Somewhat confused, she looked at Tasty,
And said, "What you doing here?"
She opened the frig and reached in the back,
Then grabbed herself a beer.

He took her hand,
And gave her a kiss.
Then she replied,
"Baby, I'm too tired for this!"

Being perplexed and all alone,
He laid with her that night.
Feeling the presence of death so near,
He received a horrifying fright!

Tasty rolled over in the middle of the night,
On the cold, damp oversized bed.
He touched her face and realized,
That she was surely dead!

He looked over on her nightstand,
And saw a syringe filled with drugs.
His heart broke in fear knowing,
There would be no more kisses and hugs.

He grieved for hours,
At the sight of his loss.
But then he knew,
He'd have to tell the boss.

When Tasty finally told her man,
That she was lifeless and dead,
He yelled at him for not watching her,
And pounded him on the head.

Another one of the girls
Then spoke up and said,
"Leave that little boy alone!"
"It's not his fault she's dead!"

The man got angry,
And threw her to the floor.
He grabbed the body by the hair,
And dragged it through the door.

Then Tasty followed them,
To the back of another room,
There he saw her body burn,
In the fireplace of doom.

Tasty broke down
In depression and sorrow.
Now he didn't care
If he ever saw tomorrow.

So back into the wild,
Tasty then went.
Without any love in his life,
And his money all spent.

Walking the streets, late one night,
A growl chilled him to the bone.
He then yelled out, "Why can't this world "
"Leave me the hell alone?

Finally, Tasty realized,
He would not be left alone.
There was no real escape,
Even when he went back home.

In his darkest hour,
Reflecting on his life,
He knew it was kill or be killed,
His relationships would end in strife.

He looked up to the sky,
And prayed from his heart,
"Is there a way out of this dark cloud?"
"God, I was doomed from the start!"

Tasty heard nothing for a few days,
And believed he was defeated.
"Why are people so damn mean,"
"And why am I so mistreated?"

Chapter 7: A Mother's Voice in the Darkness

One night Tasty heard
A very peculiar sound.
It was the voice of a mother
That was so very profound.

Scared out his wits,
He jumped out of bed.
"Are you the ghost of Sweet Mama,"
"Haunting me from the dead?"

He looked around the room,
And saw nothing but red.
He finally gave up the search;
Exhausted, he went back to bed.

A few days later,
He could not fall asleep.
Tasty heard the voice again,
And he started to weep.

A giant angel appeared that night.
She floated down like a ghost.
"Fear not child," she said,
"I'm your guide to love in the heavenly host!"

Tasty looked to the left of the angel,
Then he looked to the right.
He saw two happy children,
One was black and one was white.

Many children, around the angel,
Were all glowing with joy.
They had no burdens upon them,
Not one girl or one boy.

They were heading in a direction,
No one in the darkness could see.
Tasty scratched his head and wondered,
"Why are they so free?"

The angel said to Tasty,
"Face your fear to escape the haze."
"The people still in the darkness,"
"Remain in a zombie-like daze."

"What does that even mean!"
Tasty abruptly replied.
"Can't you see I've been abused,"
"By so many, that I've almost died!"

The angel said, "He knows who you are,"
"And even where you've been."
"Take heed to His call, child,"
"Never weep in vain again!"

Behind the angel, he saw children move,
Toward a face with an intense glow.
His silhouette shined like a sunset,
Reminding him of a place he would go.

"What is happening inside of me?"
Tasty asked the angel of light.
"Don't you see the hatred?"
"I'm haunted by spirits in the night."

The angel rose a little higher,
Her hands folded together.
"Don't worry about that, child,"
"He wants you in His love forever."

Right after that, he felt exhausted,
Then he fell asleep.
Dreaming a man knocked on his door,
He woke frightened and began to weep.

It was the knock of the angel's master,
This he could not deny.
Then and there he received the truth;
His hatred of self, had to die!

Chapter 8: Out of the Dark Cloud?

Tasty had problems letting go of the dark,
It brought him comfort in the day.
It was a place he always went to hide,
To numb his wounds and push them away.

"Crawl out of the darkness and leave it
    behind,"
Said the angel from above.
"It's the only way to escape yourself,"
"And your relationships without love."

I don't want to sound dreary,
And I don't want to sound glib,
This just one of many lives gone bad,
In the dark cloud of... "Tales from the Crib."

www.ingramcontent.com/pod-product-compliance
Lightning Source LLC
Chambersburg PA
CBHW040858120626
46551CB00001B/67